John Henry Staines was born in April 1948 in the small pottery's town of Leek in Staffordshire.

He is the second son of Robert and Sylvia Staines, and travelled with the family at the age of 9 to live in South Shields, South Tyneside, the home of his father, where he resided on and off for over 65 years.

John was diagnosed with Bipolar Affective Disorder when he was 22 and has struggled mentally to contain this illness throughout his international career as a market researcher in over 50 countries for over 500 clients.

To my late wife and business partner for 53 years, Tricia Staines. My inspiration and reason to carry on living every day.

John H Staines

BIPOLAR ADVENTURES

AUSTIN MACAULEY PUBLISHERS™

LONDON • CAMBRIDGE • NEW YORK • SHARJAH

A CIP catalogue record for this title is available from the British Library.

ISBN 9781528978002 (Paperback)
ISBN 9781398451353 (ePub e-book)

www.austinmacauley.com

First Published 2022
Austin Macauley Publishers Ltd®
1 Canada Square
Canary Wharf
London
E14 5AA

I would like to thank Austin Macauley Publishers for selecting *Bipolar Adventures* from the many aspiring writers, and for giving me a break from my troubled existence.

Chapter 1
In the Beginning

As the warm Mediterranean sun sets over Baia Caffiere on the rugged volcanic island of Ischia off the Amalfi Coast of Italy, the half-light of evening stretches across the terracotta terrace of the Continental Mare Hotel, which sits atop the cliffs of the hilly peninsular. My mind is so relaxed that memories of my childhood flood back in my sombre October mood.

I had passed my three-score years and ten fifteen months ago, the day my third grandson came into this troubled world. As I gulp my Americano coffee mulled with warm local milk to wash down my saltimbocca, the Italian version of a Parisian croque-monsieur, and then stub out my pencil-slim Cohiba Cuban mini cigar, my mind is at rest at long, long last. My mind is also further rested as a soft cool breeze satisfies my consciousness. I am trying to forget my much-troubled past.

It was a cold winter's day in Blandford Forum, Dorset, when the ambulance first came for me. I was 22 years old and had just been sacked from my dream job with SNS Communications of Poole Dorset, a town famous for its chain ferry at Sandbanks. I had studied for twelve years to obtain six GCE O levels and an Ordinary National Certificate in engineering, as well as degrees in engineering from

Sunderland Polytechnic and a Masters in Marketing and Finance from the City University of London.

Having worked studiously for my exams and completed a six-year technical apprenticeship with Alphonse Reyrolle and Company in Hebburn, prior to my burnout, I was overqualified and could not get a job anywhere for months, until Marconi Communications took me on as assistant to the commercial director at the young age of 23 in the year of our Lord 1974.

The ambulance wove through Thomas Hardy country lanes, unearthly siren sounding through the beautiful fields with their fluttering life and fairy-tale existence, taking me far from the madding crowd through *Mayor of Casterbridge* territory and beyond to two barred and unlocked gates of the hell. It was 1971, and I was about to be incarcerated for the first but not last time in my sporadic mental existence.

The hospital I was rushed to was the Dorchester psychiatric hospital at Wood End. The illness I had was known at the time as manic-depressive psychosis disorder, and I thought at the time I was doomed to a life of locks on the doors and shutters on the windows and separation from my wife, the love of my life, Tricia. After indoctrination and courses of lithium carbonate tablets and other psychiatric drugs, I endured electroconvulsive therapy torture, which involved clipping electrodes to either side of my head and passing a current through my brain until my body convulsed in pain, supposedly to clear bad memories away. I remember waking each time afterwards with a raging thirst and feeling somewhat befuddled and distant, but the tea and biscuits afterwards made me feel alive again.

Tricia always stayed by me and visited me regularly as I got progressively better over the months until my release to my home in Blandford Forum with a heavy load of medication for the rest of my life. I had no prospect of immediate work and would lack the capability of tackling any job until I had learned to read and write again—one of the many side effects of ECT, together with partial long-term memory loss.

I first met Tricia outside the post office and newsagent's shop in East Boldon Road, Cleadon Village, Tyne and Wear. She was milling round with a group of harmless teenagers looking for any place to wander; some were from over the railway lines in East Boldon. She was sweet 16, and I was an immature 16 and a half years old, and I didn't immediately fall for her, as she was rather shy. Instead I was attracted to her friend Lorraine—the talkative and forward member of their group.

Lorraine was my idol until another friend of mine, Bruce Martin, joined our group and Lorraine fell in with him; then I fell in finally with the ever-faithful Tricia. Through visiting her and her family in the front room of her father's palatial house, which was only two hundred yards down a back path near my parent's humble bungalow, our tender love would grow into a strong bond which was to last for over fifty-two years—her remaining lifetime.

Chapter 2

The Meeting

Earlier that year at a party at Lorraine's parent's home in Whitburn Village, as Bruce and Lorraine played downstairs, I took Tricia, who was devoted to me at first sight, upstairs to the parents' bedroom, where some innocent fumbling and unsatisfyingly attempted lovemaking with Tricia took place. We flushed the only unused Durex down the toilet and left for the night, only to find that Lorraine's parents had found the unused condom and were quite upset.

The next day Lorraine cleverly said that she had placed the item in the toilet in a bid to bring her mother and father together, as they were constantly bickering. The ruse worked, and she escaped the wrath of her mum and dad; we were all fortunate for her having done so. Lorraine was forgiven first by her mother and later by her father, and I breathed a sigh of relief. Phew! What an escape from Lorraine's mum and dad telling all of our parents about this mischief!

After that lucky escape, I met another girl, Jennifer. My unrequited passions with Tricia confused me, and I was drawn to Jennifer's glorious shoulder-length smooth strawberry-blonde hair and comely smile. Little did I know that my coquettish Jennifer was soon to become involved with the rakish Johnnie from across the lines in East Boldon, who I later found out had also been visiting Tricia at the stables of her stallion horse, Rocky. Her father had bought Rocky for her and stabled him in the grounds of the huge industrial plant road surfacing company he owned, Edwin Clarkson Ltd, which covered most of East Boldon Village at the time. Jennifer allowed me an innocent fumble, but I was still unsatisfied and wanted more. But it was not to come from Jennifer.

Much later, when I was travelling the world in pursuit of commercial success through my technical marketing and market research career, I was having lunch in the Holiday Inn in Hollywood, California. Tricia, who had agreed to be my fiancée, was in the UK. I started talking to a stranger in the bar, and I mentioned that my fiancée had a horse called Rocky. It wasn't many months before the first *Rocky* film came out, and I cannot help but believe that came from my conversations with a stranger in Hollywood. Who knows?

I was having another drink in the Holiday Inn bar, Hollywood, which was quite busy at the time, and the frontman of Adam and the Ants, a 1980s pop group, walked in the bar along with two or three of his group members. I was at a pretty high state with my manic depression—which would later be called bipolar disorder—and had quite a bit to drink and ended up buying everybody in the bar a free drink, which was a very expensive thing to do, even in this high state of mind. I met a chap in the bar who tried to proposition me. As he was obviously after my body and mind (ha ha!), I was convinced he was a homosexual, but I declined in time and went to bed to sleep uneasily and recover my composure alone.

This is just an example of how manic depression has manifested itself very often in my life, causing me to make rash purchases and have high ideals and delusions of grandeur. In hindsight, I've come to realise the excitement of visiting new often romantic countries and cities, very often losing sleep and living the high life mixed in with work pressures, often caused my illness to manifest itself.

Chapter 3
The Illness

I spent my youthful years near the sea in South Shields, South Tyneside. The beach my brother and I used to walk to and swim from was called Ladies Cove. It was a very rocky, and its multitudinous tidal water ebbed and flowed on the rugged coast of the North Sea, only half a mile or so away from my grandmother's house in Druridge Crescent, South Shields.

My late brother Bob was 18 months older than me, and he would take the lead. On many a summer's day we would walk across the rocks and fields and past Blackberry Hill and down to the coast, passing over an older, now disused railway line on which a locomotive called the Marsden Rattler would pull coal wagons to and from the brick kilns further up the coast, over the main highway, the coast road, and the expansive grassland known locally as Trowe Lees to the rugged coast of the North Sea.

The sea was very cold and rough at all times, particularly in the winter, which was very typical of the north-east coast. Occasionally we used to take frenzied dips, rushing into the cold, uninviting, threshing water and coming out very quickly against the dragging tide to get back out of the cold into the comparatively bracing fresh air of the north-east of England.

In later years when I was courting and my interest was in young ladies, I used to take my girlfriends down to the coast, not Ladies Cove as it was far too rough and ready but to the Marsden Grotto, a rugged but commercialised mile or so up the coast on the border of South Shields town limits, near Whitburn, which was a marvellous beach of rocks edged into by the sea and surrounding a huge rock called Marsden Rock. Access to the sea and rock-strewn beach was down a very rickety 139 steps down the cliff face and when it was working there was an electric lift which was very infrequently repaired, and which used to work occasionally. It was a marvellous atmosphere with seabirds and seagulls swooping and nesting on top of the rock leaving their dirt all over the rocks, but it was very romantic I've since been there many, many times and still do.

Over the years I've revisited Marsden Grotto a number of times with various ladies I mentioned earlier and it still has for me something of a magical existence. There is a bar/restaurant now built into the caves in the bottom of the grotto, down the staircase or lift and I've often frequented that bar which has a very romantic if wild tidally feeling.

Skipping to the other side of the world to many countries and cities some on the west coast of California, especially a place called Sausalito I found a very similar beach atmosphere with rocky coves and seagulls which I realised was a mirror image to the Marsden Grotto, but with very different people and attitudes and despite being on the other side of the world and travelling to, it had a similar atmosphere of coming home and an old traveller's saying came to mind namely if you travel around the world enough times eventually you will meet yourself.

The love of the sea for me wasn't just visual and artistic it was also enticing and when I was very young, around 24 years old, I had my first lessons in wind surfing on a reservoir in Hertfordshire near where Tricia, my now wife and I lived in Hemel Hempstead in Hertfordshire. I bought my first wind surf board as I was hooked and later whilst travelling on holidays to different countries, I took my windsurfing board to places including Corsica and the South of France. There's nothing more invigorating than feeling the power of the wind and nature of the current in the arms and legs, at what seems like break neck speed and inducing quick gusts and turns as the ever-changing wind and current patterns exhausted themselves.

But this love of windsurfing led on to a love of sailing boats and I bought my first dingy and later my first family sized sailing boat, a small Bermudan Sloop called the Sunspot. When we lived in Hemel Hempstead, we drove all the way to Suffolk to buy this 15-foot-long would you believe 4 berth sailing boat. I was told at the time that this particular boat had sailed to Norway and back, a feat which that I didn't really relish and would not have lived up to, instead I bought a mooring for the Sunspot on the Norfolk Broad's and towed it down there, and left it there in between weekends. I found that I really loved sailing, problem was the water at the Broad's was only about 5 or 6 feet deep in places, so the twin keels of the Sunspot sailing boat occasional caught up on the bottom which was a bit disconcerting as it would keel over until the wind stabilised the boat.

In a later season we moved house and I sold the Sunspot whilst still moored on the Norfolk Broads and I got paid back for just what I'd paid for it £750 in spite of the fact me and the family had used it over a number of seasons it still kept its value and held some lovely memories of Tricia and I.

Much later when we lived in Hertfordshire in the village of Boxmoor, Hemel Hempstead, I bought another boat in a feat of mania high and that was a Seafarer 275, travelling down to Hayling Island of the South coast to seal the deal. It was a seagoing boat but roughly the same size of the Sunspot but very much more modern. I used to keep it in moored in our little garden of Roughdown Lodge, Boxmoor our last of three homes which we had in Hemel Hempstead and used to tow it to all kinds of places including rivers and lakes in the South of England, even abroad and all the way to the south of France to the harbour of Cavalier Sumere on the Riviera and we sailed it to many places down the Mediterranean coast.

One of which was to a restaurant we had found when driving and it was a journey of about 3 miles, we got the restaurant and asked if we could eat and they said there was cancellation for a Bouillabaisse for 2 so Tricia and I just dived in and enjoyed the meal and the atmosphere and our eldest sons Justin and Paul, our only family at the time just enjoyed the magnificent beach, James wasn't born then and we had sailed along the rugged coast and parked our boat on the beach at the café.

When we attempted to sail back to the harbour about 3 miles back, as we left shore, a terrible wind storm blew up which I now know the locals called the Mistral which occurs in September. We were in peril and to cut a long story very short we just managed to sail the boat and keep it afloat out of water despite the cries of my two children, we all struggled for what seemed like hours for a long time back to the harbour but the harbour master told us the harbour was closed for the evening. At the height of frustration, I saw a spot, just a small space about the size of the Seafarer and squeezed the boat into it. There was a giant boat next to us in the double berth, a huge German owned yacht and the owners had to interrupt their lavish dinner and help me to berth my tiny little craft, which there was just enough room for the Seafarer.

I will never forget that day and since then none of my family have gone sailing again. We sold the Seafarer a few years later and to put an end to my seafaring days I have taken risks when I am high on life and fortunately somehow the divine forces are always with me and the trouble I got into when on the sea.

Later I bought a windsurf board from Earls Court Exhibition centre in London and had many a happy and more stable times, quite safely by myself I'm pleased to say. From then on, my sailing was limited to large ships, ferries and cruise liners. In later years without my lovely Tricia by my side I set out on a number of cruises on my own from the UK.

Chapter 4

The Loss of Tricia

Tricia contracted breast cancer and it took seven years for her to go through the various stages of deterioration, she finally died on the Thursday 29th October 2015 at 5 am in the morning. She had had several remissions and there was always hope that she would last longer, especially on my part. When the final news from the medical team came, they said she had only a few weeks to live or thereabouts and it was a shattering although expected experience to me.

I must have been to 50 or so periodic meetings with various reviews of her condition by the medical team over that period and on every other occasion I had been given by the doctors the belief that she would at least live a little longer in each case, but now I was given the ultimatum that her life was almost at an end and that she didn't have much longer to live.

There was a very different mood to the meeting and the cancer doctor took me to one side and told me of her change in condition from breast cancer to lymph node cancer to brain cancer, but if was obviously not a positive prognosis as previously, as the cancer was now untreatable.

So over the next 3 weeks Trish became a very strong person mentally and more or less arranged her own funeral, even deciding on which music she would like and the fact that it would be a humanist service, for her funeral with a speaker organised by the humanist society and through an individual consultant person which Tricia had already chosen for the service and we discussed which flowers for herself she would and would not like.

The funeral directors were Johnsons of South Shields and they were very accommodating and understanding and supportive, needless to say I was in a flat spin for those few weeks and hated the thought of the inevitable happening in a short time and it's a good job Tricia was strong, as it was her strength that got me through the last weeks.

When the day came it was all planned for and pretty predictable, I was in total shock that she had actually died even though I'd expected it for seven years, it didn't seem as if it were a real situation. I functioned partially because of my three sons who at various times visited my house in which Tricia was dying, the house I still live at in West Boldon and in turn I tried my best to stay strong for them and they themselves were supportive and stayed strong for me.

This got me through the first 24 hours of my bereavement and getting used to sleeping in an empty bed and a day or two after that helped me preparing/arranging the death certificate and the final details for the funeral.

The day of the funeral arrived and my thoughts/feelings were just to get through it so I could start to rebuild my shattered life again. It was a sunny day and we went to South Shields Crematorium, myself and my immediate family in limousines as Tricia was of course taken in her coffin in a hearse ahead of us.

The service seemed like a dream now and it went very smoothly and was quite short as Tricia's body disappeared through the curtains and that was the end for her.

Tricia's farewell reception was held at the Black Bull public house in East Boldon a quarter of a mile from mine and Tricia's home and it was very well attended by family, friends and acquaintances and was a blur to me despite the fact that I tried to thank as many people as possible for coming and for their best wishes and condolences and memories of Tricia.

The next thought I had in the oblivion of my feelings, was what on earth I would do with the ashes which were delivered by the funeral director in a cardboard container and I discussed this at times with Justin, Paul and James and each of them had different ideas as to what they would like to do with their mam's ashes.

Later on James came with me to a holiday park I had been to with Tricia and had happy times with in Filey, owned by Hoseasons and we scattered some of her ashes on a rose bush just outside the terraced House that Tricia and I had shared a number of times for various holidays.

Paul had his own ideas and requested a couple of tablespoons full of ashes and he placed them in a little heart shaped pouch for his own special memories. Justin arranged for his share of his mam's ashes to be buried under a rose bush in West Park, Boldon where he often took his dog for a walk, and arranged for memorial plaque to identify them. I keep my share of the ashes in the next bedroom to mine and have yet to scatter them but in the meantime, they are an extra memory of Tricia for me in the home which I shared with her for more than 20 years.

Chapter 5

The Depression

Gradually I came to terms that I was alone and would probably be so for the rest of my life as I couldn't at that time even dream of a possibility of finding a replacement for Tricia, but over the months and now years that followed I felt that I had sort solace with female company and made some very good female friends over the years, not necessarily girlfriends, and had some new experiences in life which however were only shadows of the experiences Id had before Tricia finally went. Nevertheless, these relationships were interesting and took up some of the weight of time I had on my hands, as I was in retirement from the day my wife/partner/best friend and companion passed away.

Looking backwards I was amazed that I hadn't gone into severe clinical depression as one part of the cycle of a manic depressive. When I lost Tricia I was very depressed and bereaved and was totally disorientated, my family were worried about me and obviously with my medical history that I have, that I would go into deep depression and not return out of it via suicide, but as it happened days became weeks, weeks became months and months became years and when I was talking to my sons about my loneliness, they suggested well why don't you get a dog for company as you're in the house by yourself all the time with the 2 cats which I'd inherited and were sort of still Tricia's cats.

I thought I would like a small Jack Russell probably a bitch because Tricia and I had as part of our lives together had a Jack Russell cross called Jackie and also a bitch and very faithful and very good company around the house she was. So I looked on the internet for Jack Russell puppies and found there were lots available but none local to me in Boldon, also they were hundreds of pounds which rather put me off as I wasn't prepared to pay that.

Coincidence or my luck took a turn for the better and the following Friday my eldest son Justin was in the Black Bull pub and a lady approached him who I now know as Leslie and said to him do you know anyone who needs or wants a Jack Russell dog, he replied he would talk to me about it and get back to her. Anyway that is how Olive came into my life, a beautiful 3-year-old at the time Jack Russell bitch and we found that it is because Leslies family who lived next door to the Black Bull in a haberdashery, had at the time 4 dogs and Olive wasn't getting on with any of them and that she needed to find a home very quickly. Justin described my circumstances to Leslie who approached him in the Black Bull public house and asked if he knew anyone interested and could meet up in her shop next door. So I went down to the shop to meet the dog and it was love at first sight she was lovely and we got on like a house on fire.

I took Olive for a walk around the block on Leslies suggestion to see how I got on with her and I was very attracted to her and asked Leslie if I could take her home for a couple of hours to see how she got on with my 2 cats Scamp and Spot, which were Tricia's earlier acquisitions as she was very fond of cats.

3 years later Olive has completely settled down from the wild child she was with Leslie and is marvellous company and is of a lovely nature and I just count my lucky stars, that she is named after my late wife Patricia Olive, again for which I will be eternally grateful.

Chapter 6
Yorkshire

Up to my loss of Tricia and my subsequent retirement in 2015 we took two last holidays together in the painful knowledge that they would probably be our last ones before hospitalization and hospice stays as an inpatient for Tricia.

The first was a holiday in Filey with Tricia in April 2015, we were booked through Hoseasons holiday parks for a holiday home near Filey, North Yorkshire. Called 'Escape to the country'. We had a lovely week in a semi detected holiday villa on a small site of around 100 properties with a bar/pub/restaurant on site I think was called the Brigadier.

There were various facilities on site including archery and ducks and we saw quite a few animals including seals, as we were close to the beach about 10 minutes' walk away and very many seagulls. The site was within easy reach by car to Filey itself and further down the coastal road to Scarborough in north Yorkshire. The road to the south led to small coastal villages which were very picturesque and eventually led to Filey, Scarborough to Bridlington and then to Skegness just inside Lincolnshire.

The site we were on was mainly terraced villas there was a roundabout in the middle with the houses surrounding, on the east site adjacent there were mobile homes and chalets of various types and the whole atmosphere was of a varied and interesting ambiance. We enjoyed little trips driving along the north Yorkshire moors and winding country lanes down to various villages which each generally had their own rustic public house, and we had a couple of drinks and some very nice meals at each one of them, all peculiar but quaint villages and pubs.

Trish's health was good but deteriorating as her breast cancer and lymphoma cancer had advanced, but it didn't stop us having a good time and enjoying life in the Yorkshire countryside.

Quite a bit later when Tricia was declining and her mobility was more of an issue, we booked an impromptu holiday in Santorini, one of the Greek islands we hadn't been to before, which would have been recommended by many people. We had a holiday of sorts reflecting on our many memories on many Greek islands including this lovely volcanic island, but Tricia by then was suffering to a large extent with her immobility and could only walk short distances with the aid of her walking sticks which dictated our movements to stay close to our apartment and the town centre which was not very far away, which was basic, small but adequate, as she could move around relatively easily and make the best of a unsatisfactory situation. We managed to get out and about as we were just walking and strolling and had no hire car but we still managed to get to 2 or 3 of the local hostelries and enjoyed a late summer early autumn holiday, as the whole resort was shutting down for winter.

That was obviously the last holiday I had with Tricia and she with me and at least it took our mind of the very many consultations and medical meetings that we had to go through in the last year or so of her life and we made it there and we made it back unscathed. That's all my memory retains of what was a very difficult but therapeutic holiday with Tricia.

Chapter 7
New Beginnings

Following the funeral and my general disorientation that I felt at Trish's death. In March/April 2016 my youngest son James kindly volunteered to take me on holiday to see if we could start to repair our shattered lives. And we went where to, guess it, yes, Filey on the Hoseasons site this time taking some of Tricia's ashes at which we scattered a few on the rose bush next to the house Tricia and I had enjoyed many times.

In 2016 nine month later when I had recovered my composure slightly, I booked a holiday, a cruise to the Mediterranean to Greece, and on board ship, through passing in the corridor a number of times I worked up the courage to ask a young Persian lady Anabella would she like to go for a coffee, she said yes straight away even though she was many years younger than me. I needed the exercise of massaging my heartache away. Anabella and I on the cruise went on some of the various Grecian islands forming a growing friendship. I found out during the coffee that she lived on the west side of London and was an accountant she had a business mainly servicing the accountancy and financial consultancy needs of restaurants over London. She was a lovely young lady aged about 35 and very open and honest and kind. I realised that we had so much in common, despite the fact that she had departed Iran with her father and mother, under very difficult circumstances and had built her own home and was in constant touch with various uncles and aunties, but she had been let down badly by her previous boyfriend, who she had just grown out of love with in her very busy life.

She was very good looking, smaller than I with large almond eyes and she was very intelligent as anyone could tell from first meeting her and I assumed that from all the property she owned around Europe was quite wealthy. But she was still looking for happiness and in my broken heart over Tricia I had managed to convince her, as we kept in touch almost daily by text, to come up to the North East of England by train from London. I encouraged it and took her to various places, including one of my favourite places on earth which is Marsden Grotto in South Shields, Justin my eldest son, Andrea his fiancée, she and I shared a drink at the bar at the grotto out on the terrace, when she was quite amazing because she was picking up stones from the beach for her back garden and she bought half of the presents from the Grotto mini shop to take home with her as keepsakes.

I forgot to mention that when we met in London, I had a national coach holiday which I had arranged to go down to London to hopefully see her, we had a couple of drinks together, although she was not a heavy drinker. We had a walk round Canary Wharf where we were looking at the various city businesses in that area and we were impressed by how many publishing companies there were as well as financial organizations. We went for a couple of drinks here and there and from the hotel in London, whose names escapes me, we spent a few hours together and she got back on the tube for her 30-minute journey to where she lived at and I went back to the hotel, there was no hanky-panky or funny business as I respected her too much too even bring that subject up whilst she was bouncing back from her previous relationships, it didn't seem gentlemanly to press her too hard.

Anabella came to the north east and to my surprise she found it most impressive she loved the little terrace houses within the and coal mining villages and little pubs along the Coast Road from South Shields to Whitburn and Seaburn in Sunderland and we had a lovely time. Although it was always in the back of my mind was that I would never replace Tricia and she was not her substitute. However, as I booked her in to Friendly Hotel in Boldon nearby my home, we did have an occasion to have a drink in the hotel as she was very tired from the journey. Next evening, she invited me back to the hotel for a drink and we ended up in her bedroom and the inevitable happened. It was like a therapy and I didn't realise it was doing me so much good. Days, weeks and months later I suddenly felt revived and happy I'd met her knowing we would never meet again but just thankful for the company and companionship and self-esteem she had given back to me.

When Anabella went back to London on the train, she mentioned in her text that she was going to see plot of land in Sweden and was considering building a house there, where she met a young Swede whose name I cannot bring to mind, and fell in love with him replacing me in her affections. We kept in touch and I encouraged her to have a good time, a good laugh and be careful, and she messaged me over the years and we still remain the very best of friends today.

More recently she texted me and said she had fallen in love again, this time with a young school teacher called Gavin and was hoping to marry him. So, with all of my counselling over the years, touched with love has resulted in my best lady friend finding happiness despite the power of estate of her finances, when her business collapsed due to the Covid 19 Pandemic.

I wish them both good health and happiness and children to bless their relationship to carry on her family line.

Chapter 8
Pole to Pole

I hadn't really used my technical qualifications in electrical and electronic engineering, during my early career which was mainly marketing and sales but I had a hankering to do something about that, starting in the fall of 1977.

I had etched out a career in marketing and market research provisionally for technical clients and had quite a few of them in my early days, under the name of John Staines Associates, abbreviated to JSA, which was mainly research for marketing of companies with relatively technical products and services. I ended up with a range of 100's of clients, over the years including the UK Government and the US Government, USA Department of Commerce, both of whom I developed good relations with due to my enthusiastic but pragmatic approach to relatively technical areas and projects in sovereign countries.

My bipolar disorder, which to many people would be a grave disadvantage for commercial success, was in my case on numerous occasions a silver lining, because the high cycle and low black lethargy from depression and back to creative mania over seasons. This means that at some times in my existence I became very, very creative, while on an upwards cycle to the highs and unfortunately, on the lower cycle to the depression. I just started all over again with a new business strategy and gradually rose out of it to form a new career, being quite sure that eventually another cycle would put me on my beloved highs.

When I was high or going high, I found I could enjoy the quality of life in spades, travel, good food, female company and most of all a challenge and I'd set myself a one with starting off my own business in computer hardware and software development. To fund this business, I undertook market research for various companies all over the world which was normally funded by Government sources, which I had to seek to develop and make proposals for, also private sector publishers internationally.

It occurred to me that sometime in the market research process that there was space for another enterprise in the UK, Europe and North America, which combined research and economic marketing, so I set up a company with dual purpose in the name of Datacapture Limited based in my home at the time of Hemel Hampstead, Hertfordshire. Whilst being mainly a theorist in electronics I had a yearning to actually put a simple theory into practice my experience with a number of other data acquisition and data logging companies such as Fluke in the US and Microdata and Cristie Electronics in the UK, all of whom I had worked for in my much-varied and travelled international and technical career to date.

The purpose of a data Logger was to capture electronic data on many things, but mostly on the weather and environmental conditions and to put together a tool to develop it, the DATABLOCK™ for the Natural Environmental

Research Council who funded and controlled 17 Research Institutes in and around Britain.

I placed an advert in the London Evening Standard and within a month I had four engineers with various disciplines in electronic engineering, who were all prepared to work in their spare time (part-time) to develop the concept into a rugged flexible electronic box centred around a microprocessor to control time and function against a heartbeat pulse, scanning all input channels once a second controlled by a crystal electronic clock with 16 channels in binary steps. This was the first totally solid-state device with no moving parts of its kind.

The finished product which took 2 years starting off in the summer house of my home Roughdown Lodge in Hemel Hempstead, Hertfordshire in which we would meet weekly for an hour or so in the summerhouse to progress the development from drawing board to the finished DATABLOCK™ and the satellite remote DATABRICK™ hardware and software in around one thousand components and its own micro computer chip, the box/chassis were all made of aluminium for lightness and aversion to corrosion from moisture.

Most of the kit was sub-contracted for manufacture and my original partner, Edward, from Cambridge Trinity College, and I approached many financial organizations to try to fund the project, and after 2 years of development and trying to get a financial backer, we'd just about to be given up until we conducted a launch of the products at the Wembley Exhibition Centre, London. The press stands were very kind to us and the Electronics Times headlined the event and us as

"DATACAPTURE™ Stars at Wembley", on the front page of their newspaper the very next day.

Having tried to reach finance for almost 2½ years on the project which was funded entirely from loans and out of my own pocket, within one week we were contacted by two venture capital companies, one was Norwich Union and the other was Midland Bank Venture Capital Ltd. They offered £150,00.00 venture capital money spread over a year and a half and then the 1st half payment hit the bank within days, for the first time in our lives we were in positive funds.

The 1st £75,000.00 was paid into our bank and with my manic tendency I had already began to spend it on Company business, booklets, literature and components and within a few months of development, we had moved from our high street single office to a plush large factory unit ½ a mile away on an industrial estate, still in Hemel Hempstead. Our purchasing power in components and sub-contract arrangements improved overnight as a series of prototypes majoring in scientific instruments for which at the time were booming and in great demand from Government organizations.

It lasted a year with production and the DATABLOCK™ prototype which copied the human brain and a pulse of roughly once per second close to the human heartbeat and a scanning speed. It was market leader for roughly a year or so later until a Canadian company copied our ideas and flooded the market with a more rapidly scanning product which also found additional markets in faster applications of data acquisition.

Before that intervention we gained many clients and customers for DATABLOCK™ including our largest customer which was the UK Government's British Antarctic Surveys which were funded through the Natural Environmental Research Council and they bought 9 DATABLOCK's™ at £10,000.00 each over 2 years, most of which went to the south pole and contributed to the discovery of the hole in the earth's ozone layer which was a major scare to environmentalists at the time.

We had funds coming in and another customer was British Petroleum who were researching oil sources and environmental issues at the north pole to record topographical information in the Arctic compatible with oil exploration. It was mainly the south pole that our markets were developed by ourselves and we had no external partner or large organization to depend on but we had conquered both the north pole and the south pole electronically speaking.

Unfortunately for us Midland Bank Venture Capital Ltd was taken over by HSBC and no further funds for the 2nd half of project were forthcoming, so our cash dried up and in December 1984 we were broke. In retrospect however we had achieved a significant advance in science instruments over the seven years that DATACAPTURE™ Limited had operated and had managed to net sales of almost 30 DATABLOCK's™ around the world including as far as Sweden, Germany, Ireland and United States.

I had a love of travel which I used quite often to further my market research career having accumulated and gained in depth experience of other cultures, politics and geography, so in retrospect this was a very worthwhile exercise and one that I would repeat readily, if I could spot another gap in the market place. These events enabled to me to develop other multi technical marketing business as a consultant, which would be another feather in my cap.

The entire DATACAPTURE™ Ltd Company was sold to a company called Conlec in Sheffield who took our stock of components and any information we could give them on marketing etc, but within four months they were also bust and liquidated.

DATABLOCK™ and to be honest THE DATABRICK™ remote unit which was never fully developed was a quirk of bipolar imagination and fate and anyone in this situation had to just carry on and look for the next opportunity.

After 2 years of barely existing in our Hertfordshire home Roughdown Lodge, Midland bank finally took steps to sell our beloved home and by moving back up north, we had returned many debts back to them.

We moved into a more or less derelict 13 roomed terrace house in Victoria Avenue, Bishop Auckland, which we renamed Prospect House and started a technology forecasting and Marketing research company called Prognosis Ltd. It was a consultancy, research and projections company for various clients in the area forecasting into the future, which lasted a further nine years until we returned further north from County Durham to Boldon to our current family home, partly because our older relatives needed support assistance in our aging local family.

West Boldon my current home is a stone's throw from Cleadon Village, Tyne & Wear where I had been brought up for most of my early life and where my father a very successful engineer, who died a month before Tricia 5 years ago, lived.

I thank God for the family support I gained during my Father and Tricia's demise in a quiet friendly region of the North East of England, where we managed to eke out an existence enriched by our former glories and memories as a much liked and honest government research contractor.

Chapter 9
The Early Years

I was born on the 21st April 1948 the Queen's birthday and my father was born on the 4th August 1920 the Queen mothers' birthday. I had a difficult upbringing within a very poor but hard-working family and throughout my childhood, whilst bonuses and luxury were never a factor, I always knew I was loved by my mother Sylvia and father Robert and I had a brother called Bob who was 18 months older than me and his birthday was on the 1st December 1945, which was the Queens Jubilee and we were well provided for.

The town of my birth was Leek in Staffordshire. A town which was south of the potteries and was within the borders of the Staffordshire textile industry as well, but was surrounded by beautiful countryside in particular hills namely called Leachy Hills. I was told by my uncle Clive that at one time had been the territory of bison animals, deer and stags, but then Clive was fond of romanticizing at heart. Clive was my eldest uncle on my mothers' side and he had a younger brother called Rex.

My father was stationed in the area as a de-mobbed army corporal and met my mother in a nightclub in Leek where she was the club's singer and their romance blossomed from there. They were married in South Shields my father's home town some years later when his mother and father, John Henry Staines – who I was named after – and mother Elizabeth lived.

My elder brother Bob followed in my father's footsteps into engineering, which he was very good at inheriting my father's engineering skills, determination and never say die attitude, but unfortunately he died aged 51 from cancer of the bowel and had a very short time in this world as it was very difficult to diagnose in those days. Bob and I whilst we fought as children were the best of friends in his short adulthood and he was married for the 2nd time to Sylvia, the same name as my mother. I miss him every day as my older sibling.

My uncles on my mother's side were Rex and Clive who came to live with us in Crewe, Cheshire in a council house as both of their parents were killed during or shortly after the 2nd world war. Rex and Clive came to live with Bob, myself, my mum and dad in Crewe where my father was working as an engineer at Rolls Royce Aero Engines, where he had been employed up to his call up to the army in 1944. He travelled with the invading forces to Germany as a tank wireless operator capturing Italian tanks on the way and parking his own tank in Munich, Germany at the end of the 2nd world war.

The exact place of birth for me and Bob was 101 Junction Road, Leek, Staffordshire, which was my mother's family home, which was close to the railways. It was a small but cosy two bedroomed terraced council house but somehow, we all seemed to squeeze in pretty comfortably and accept the cramped conditions, mainly because we had not known any difference in the beginning in our lives.

There was no TV of course just a radio and various squabbles took place between mainly Bob and Rex and on one occasion Rex took Bob to task for some childhood skirmish in which he took a hammer to Bobs lovely train set, but most of the time we generally got on okay as there were four very different male children and adolescences, together with mum and dad. We had outings in my dad's car a Riley Flying 9 to various places in the region including to the Rising Sun Public House, Nantwich and others as a special treat and those were very happy times.

Bob and I, mum and dad also used to go to the Rolls Royce Country Club where my mum and dad loved to dance and were very accomplished dancers. The treat of the evening for Bob and I was that we sat outside of the Riley while mum and dad danced was a bottle of pop and a packet of crisps each in the car, probably the happiest times of my live so far.

When I was eight my parents decided along with several other couples and families to immigrate to a new life to Kitchener, Toronto, Canada as my father and his colleagues had engineering skills and experience which would be invaluable to a relatively new country in which the economy was burgeoning and Immigration was quite popular from the UK at that difficult time in Britain after the war.

We travelled up north to South Shields, Tyne & Wear where my father's family lived to say goodbye to them before emigrating and my father flying to Toronto, to start to set up a home and get a job and develop an existence in Canada.

We went up north to say goodbye to his family, who was my grandmother and grandfather Staines who had seven boys and one surviving girl (Aunty Betty). They lived in South Shields at 21 Druridge Crescent, Horsley Hill, staying in my grandmothers' house in 2 bedrooms. Most of the uncles had left home by then, but we kept in touch with them frequently visiting my grandmother's house, for about three months until my father's flight was due as a pathfinder.

Unfortunately, my father fell ill or had changed his mind about emigrating and couldn't fly on his pioneer flight with his mates from Rolls Royce, so we ended up staying with my grandmother and grandfather for some time. Bob and I went to Horsley Hill Junior school while Rex and Clive went to a more senior school in the area.

Through all of this hard work my dad managed to save to afford and put a deposit down on a new bungalow in Cleadon Village in a very desirable area. When we visited the housing site frequently, we counted almost every brick until the house was completed.

We moved in to the two-bedroom bungalow in Cleadon namely East Boldon Road. In the second bedroom were Bob and I, Rex and Clive slept facilitated by 2 sets of up and down single bunk beds, which was very cramped but they were the Halcion days, as the whole family were together. This location was within easy motorcycling distance of Reyrolle's in Hebburn my father's employer, and later to be my employer in which my six-year technical apprenticeship was commissioned and from 16 to 21 years old when I met my future wife Tricia Clarkson, who lived with her wealthy parents Roland and Joan Clarkson, 150 yards away from my parents' bungalow in a palatial semidetached house in the desirable Whitburn Road in Cleadon Village.

At long last it appeared that my luck was about to change for the better after a long and protracted start to my life, when at this stage a different life began when I first met Tricia's family.

Chapter 10
Cruising the World

After the cruise to the Mediterranean and Greece on which I'd met Anabella, my appetite was whetted for cruises and holidays and as my father had died at the ripe old age of 95 and left me and all of the surviving family well provided for.

The first cruise I took to the Caribbean sailing from Southampton and across the Atlantic Ocean, which was quite an ordeal, and took some six days to reach Barbados. I met a Lady from Filey called Sue and we kept each other's company all across the Atlantic until we reached Barbados. We cruised around 10 of the Caribbean islands, the most likable I found was Antigua, we also called in at St Kitts, the Virgin Islands, British Basseterre, not to mention Phillipsburg St Maarten, Grand Turk and the appropriately named St Johns in Antigua, St Vincent and back to Barbados.

At that time of year namely January which was one of the winter months in the UK, instead of the freezing cold we were bathed in glorious sun shine most of the cruise, with the occasional overcast day.

My next holiday was a flight from Newcastle to Tenerife for a singles week in March 2018, there were five singles plus myself and as a first experience of such a holiday I found it very good, but there were no romances between the singles as most of them seemed to be pretty well hung up on the own lives back in the UK.

The only drawback of that the holiday was the location as it was at the northern point of Tenerife namely at Puerto de la Cruz adjacent to the volcano Mount Tide, which led to a very damp and rainy climate for the week I was there. But we travelled on one occasion down south down to Las Americas, on the south coast, only a journey of 60 kilometres and we were basking in sunshine unlike the north of the island. The whole week was enjoyable and I found that in the company of others, who were in the same boat as myself more or less, a certain degree of concord and having to push myself initially into conversations and tolerate each and every one of the singles hang-ups and quibbles, but apart from that I really enjoyed the time I spent in Tenerife.

Probably my most enjoyable cruise I've had apart from the two I've had to the Caribbean, was to the Balkans and Russia sailing from Southampton. It was certainly an eyeopener to see how the Russians lived in St Petersburg, which was a beautiful city with fantastic history and we were met with nothing but friendship and courtesy from all the Russians that we mingled with. The height of that was a visit to the Winter Palace which was a massive, magnificent and ornate structure which was entirely decorated indoors with gold and gold leaf.

I met one of my friends from the Caribbean cruise, Sue who had booked on the same cruise as me, which she modesty tells me was by coincidence rather than preferred choice and it was nice to have some company from someone who I knew well and helped with conversations with the other singletons.

Other stops on the cruise were Tallinn Estonia, Travemunde Germany, Renne Denmark, Stockholm Sweden, Goatland Sweden and the Grandeur and majesty of the Kiel Canal Germany to Holland on the return trip to Southampton.

The whole cruise thing was over for me as I had more or less spent all my small inheritance on cruises as I'd been on five in the space of three years and wouldn't have changed a single moment on any of my cruises or holidays. My weakening financial status on my bank account was more or less gone after a number of bipolar episodes on the cruises. Also, my short cruises were very much more economic than the intercontinental cruises I'd enjoyed previously.

To the end of 2018 I met at lady called Susie at my local post office, while out for my morning walk and coffee with Olive my dog. Susie was an ex-model and despite being just a few months older than me and we got on really well in the early days and met quite frequently for a drink of coffee or tea in various places close to us, and she lived only two miles away from me. She had been married four times and published the book Sue Who, which I read avidly from cover to cover, nevertheless our year together on and off became short lived because of my bipolar antics and she moved on to other men with my best wishes and her preferences.

In 2019 I had repeated the whole Caribbean trip again except for this time flying from Newcastle to Barbados and picking up the ship in Bridgetown. It was very much a pleasant re-visit of the various island's I'd already explored previously but nonetheless was just as enjoyable as the other times. That was my last cruise because as I mentioned my bank account was becoming depleted and I had to set aside funds for my retirement at the age of 73.

Prior to Covid I took a holiday to Italy namely Ischia an island off the Naples Bay and thoroughly enjoyed it. Again, this was a singles holiday and there were only the four of us but we got on really well and similarly to previous singles holiday in Tenerife, where each person were very much preoccupied with their own lives and no romances took place, except I'd fallen in love with a plot of land which was the crumbling Villa Piano, which was for sale by a local agent located on top of a mountainous hill to which the only access was by a motor scooter, but would of made a glorious restaurant as it over looked the islands of Capri and Ana Capri and was steeped in romance and history. In my bipolar artistic fashion, I imagined a restaurant being built there, although heaven knows how the building materials etc. would have to make their way up a ten-minute journey zig zagging up the mountainous terrain in Piaggio vehicles, but nevertheless it was magnificent.

Another holiday I had, which was for family reasons was to Northern Ireland flying from Newcastle to Belfast in September of this year (2020). My youngest son James had found a lady over there named Michaela and they had a baby called Jude who is the light of James's, Michaela and my lives. Michaela has two daughters from previous relationships namely Holly and Katie Marie and James has more or less adopted the two girls as well, because he sees them most of the time when he is visiting Jude who is now almost 3 years old. I'm extremely proud of James as he's turned into a caring family man and a fine figure of a young man, having travelled the globe himself for his various businesses previously.

Chapter 11
The Future

And now for the theory of the illness I was diagnosed with at the young age of 22 which has blighted my life ever since causing me to make and lose at least 3 financial fortunes over my life to date. Nevertheless, provided me with great ecstasies throughout the highs and depression and despair during the lows, which for the purpose of this book the reader can learn from and hopefully avoid such cycles themselves or for their loved ones.

Below is a description/explanation of the characteristics of someone who is suffering from bipolar disorder, which in many cases is simply an imbalance in the blood stream which can be corrected to some extent by lithium carbonate amongst other medication, as I have been taking for the last 50 years, which has proved successful for me to live a relatively ordinary life by suppressing some of the highs and lows in my mood swings, but not all.

Simply put bipolar disorder is defined as:

"A mental disorder caused by structural and functional changes in the brain or changes in genes. Affected individuals experience episodes of depression and episodes of mania.

Bipolar disorder lasts for a lifetime, with treatments aiming at managing the symptoms by psychotherapy and medication."

Symptoms can last over a period of few weeks, months, or even years.

Manic phase is characterised by:

- *Extreme happiness, hopefulness, and excitement*
- *Irritability, anger, and hostile behaviour*
- *Restlessness*
- *Rapid speech*
- *Poor concentration and judgment*
- *Increased energy*
- *Less need for sleep*
- *Unusually high sex drive*
- *Setting unrealistic goals*
- *Paranoia*

The depressive phase may include:

- *Sadness and crying*
- *Feelings of hopelessness, worthlessness, and guilt*
- *Loss of energy*
- *Loss of interest in everyday activities*
- *Trouble concentrating and making decisions*
- *Irritability*
- *Need for more sleep or sleeplessness*
- *Change in appetite*
- *Weight loss/gain*
- *Suicidal thoughts and attempts at suicide*

Patients may feel normal, without any symptoms, in between episodes of mania and depression.

For further information please see website
www.bipolaruk.org

I sincerely hope that when you have read this book you find it entertaining, stimulating, in some ways humorous, mind set changing and hopefully useful, especially if you personally know or suspect anyone who might be suffering from bipolar disorder or someone who you know amongst family and friends, then as a guide to help their life make sense and achieve cumulative success and coping with tragedy stoically, but most importantly especially and successfully in a very taxing new circumstance which is the challenging contra virus phase of the world's evolution.

Chapter 12
Valletta Cruise

After my father and wife Tricia died in 2015 and my inheritance came from my father eventually over the period 2016-2019. I took to cruising as a single person and in total booked, and went on 5 cruises as my bipolar took effect over the years after my first mental breakdown and hospitalization. when I was 22-years-old and I was not at that time short of money, I was no stranger to booking expensive holidays when I was in a high mood and enjoying the high life exasperated by my bipolar mood swings on luxury cruises when on board ship. When I was as high as the proverbial kite and money was virtually no object unlike later years when my inheritance was almost gone.

The first cruise I booked and went on involved a flight from Newcastle airport to Malta's capital Valletta, where I had previously arranged an apartment two days prior to joining the cruise ship, and two days after returning from the seven day cruise, amongst other places in the Greek islands and mainland Greece, namely Kefalonia, Zante, Crete and Athens which I enjoyed immensely and didn't find that travelling as a single man was too difficult, because in retrospect, I had great confidence at most times as I was in a high mood swing.

Valletta was beautiful but compact capital city of Malta with its winding streets of tall terraced houses, some four or five stories high on either side of its winding terraced streets, houses, offices and apartments of unique character, verging on Italian architecture combined with Greek character. My fourth floor apartment in the main street was small, but comfortable, and also full of character with far reaching views of Valletta and Malta.

The Maltase people were very friendly and once we got over the language barrier, they could speak generally in good English and with my little Italian we managed to communicate well in the street cafes, bars and restaurants.

The food and drinks were delicious and were with very Mediterranean in slant and I took to wandering/rambling the oldie worldly winding an generally busy terraced streets without apprehension for my time in Valletta and on tours I made from Valletta to the Victoria Island, part of Malta, around which I noted that the English in particular were welcome because of the very close relationship we had forged with the Maltese during the second world war and that relationship was evident in the history of the island and the islanders.

The cruise was around about half a dozen of the Greek islands and took place in glorious sunshine typical of the Mediterranean and the Ionian Sea with blue skies and calm blue seas all the way on the cruise liner with every imageable luxury and legal and moral activity on board. I had booked the cruise and apartment through Fred Olsen Cruise Lines and they were helpful, friendly and masterful mainly because of the tremendous facilities for just about every pastime, not just eating and drinking, which I did with great enjoyment but also in the accommodation and friendliness of the staff on board ship, who could go to any ends to make their guests welcome and happy.

My pleasures were multiplied by the effects of a Bipolar high and this lasted long after the return trip when I flew back to Newcastle airport from Malta and got back home from my latest singles adventure, which I look back on even today in 2021 with great warmth of memories and nostalgic beliefs. In particular, the warmth and welcoming nature to the English of the Maltase people, who went out of their way to make me welcome and share their islands with me.

The cruise around the Ionian Sea and into the Aegean Sea for the docking at Athens was my first experience of cruising, and I would recommend it to anybody particularly those people who are like me and who were left alone and single after bereavement. It was just the tonic I needed after the loss of my late wife Tricia, who had enjoyed holidays in Greece and the Greek islands over the 52 years we were together. It was almost like being at home with her and brought back very many pleasant memories of her, despite the fact I still miss her badly and savour all memories of her which were brought back by the cruise.

Chapter 13
Pre-Bipolar Years

At the tender age of sixteen, I applied for, and was accepted for a job as a laboratory assistant with Bitulac, a chemical company just quarter of a mile away from my then home with my parents near Cleadon Village. At that time, however, I was to be with Bitulac for only a month or so because of an incident that happened in the laboratory.

When I came in one morning to find that the Laboratory manager Mr McDonald had tried to commit suicide by connecting all of the gas pipes in the lab with tubes into his office and when I found him, he was lying prostrate by his desk; so my quick thinking raised the alarm and first of all I told the other two apprentices who were just arriving at the same time as me, and together we tried to turn off the gas supply and opened the window in his office to let out the gas and we noticed thankfully that he was still breathing although laboured and so in order to save him we manhandled him through the door of his office to the outside path and had a difficult time unbuttoning his shirt collar which was secured by a tie pin as was the style at that time in the sixties, but we managed somehow and called for an ambulance which arrived only minutes later and took him to hospital, I am pleased to say he survived the ordeal and made a full recovery.

I later found out that a consignment, namely a tanker full of paint from the factory had gone hard within the tankers' storage area and so not only had the paint been lost but also the ship was lost, and the lab manager had taken this disaster onto his own shoulders and was blaming himself for the loss, hence his suicide bid. Fortunately, because of the quick thinking by myself and my fellow trainees we saved his life.

When my father heard news of this, he stopped me going back to Bitulac and although I had barely started my career with them, advised me to resign and he got me an interview at the large electrical engineering company, he was working for in Hebburn, Tyneside namely A Reyrolle & Co, as a potential apprentice. I went through all of the interview's procedures and tests and passed and was awarded a place there for a six-year apprenticeship scheme, including training at Hebburn Technical College, on a block release basis, until I was 18-years-old and passed my Ordinary National Electrical Engineering certificate.

The apprenticeship comprised of spending three months training at various departments within the factory of Reyrolle, starting off in the apprentice training school and learning the rudiments of mechanical engineering using basic hand tools to produce an apprentice training block involving lots of filling/cutting and trimming of a small block of metal and various parts which had to fit into various shaped cut-outs in the block very precisely, almost to a few thousand of an inch. This took up the first month of my training at Reyrolle and thereafter, I spent three months each at various other departments of the 11,000 men and women's factory to learn as a technical apprentice, different aspects of electrical and mechanical engineering on my block release course which was to last another 3 years. Including spending terms at Sunderland Polytechnic now named Sunderland University to gain my BSc in Electrical and Electronic Engineering.

When I was 18, I was offered a place for 1 month at the Eskdale Outward Bound Mounting School in the Lake District as part of my apprenticeship and training. This I was keen to do and spent a month, mostly fell-walking and other physical training, climbing over around a dozen peaks and undertaking circuit training and running around the lake. Tarn as it was called locally at the mountain school, which was followed by a quick dip in the water and by then we were in September the temperature wasn't too bad, but apparently even in the winter students would be encouraged to dip in the cold waters and I had heard that sometimes the ice had to be broken up by the instructors for the students to take their dip. Overall restrictions were at the mountain school such as no smoking, no drinking and no associating with the opposite sex and these restrictions were maintained vehemently. For part of the training at the mountain school was circuit training which was the hardest physically work I've ever done in my life and has never been repeated since.

Fortunately, the month went quickly as it was not the holiday that I and the other students had been led to believe and I was proud to receive my certificate of completion of the Outward Bound course at Eskdale Mountain School, but one incident stuck in my mind when I was accompanied by a patrol of some eight students to climb a range of peaks on one expedition which took place under those very hot conditions, and I came down with heat exhaustion for which the only cure at the time and place was for me to be left behind at base camp by myself and eat porridge laced with salt to treat the over sweating of my body. I was left with two small tents called bivouacs and a camping stove called a primus and was deserted by the rest of the patrol who went off to climb mountains.

So as dully instructed I lit, the primus and proceeded to heat up some porridge laced with salt but unfortunately the stove which was known for being very unpredictable, burst into flames and set fire to my tent. So in my groggy state I rushed down to the nearby stream and back to the flaming tent and poured water over the flames without effect, at the same time blowing six sharp whistles the sign for SOS until I had put out the fire, but I badly burnt my hands on the hot aluminium tent poles whilst pulling them apart to save my belongings in the tent.

I waited for the 30 minutes or so, but it took a while for one of the instructors to walk down one of the mountains to the camp. Not much was left of the camp or said about my predicament until the final evening of the outward-bound course which was a concert with various sketches put on by each of the patrol of groups of eight or ten students. One of the patrols which took the micky out of my predicament, as I had been in a patrol called the Watkins, saying they viewed Watkins patrol burning with enthusiasm as usual. This created a howl of laughter and I've never lived it down until I got back home from the mountain school!

Chapter 14

The Caribbean

I had two separate bipolar highs over two years from 2017 till 2019 during which times I booked and took two cruises the 1st one from Southampton which I flew to from Newcastle airport on the Flybe airline with their short distance propeller aero planes and joined the cruise ship Ventura under Carnival lines in Southampton docks. First of all cruising to Madeira which I had visited previously with my late wife Tricia and loved the island, and then we sailed from Madeira all the way across the Atlantic Ocean to Barbados which took six days and nights cruising but there was plenty to occupy me on board the ship to pass the time in luxury.

The Atlantic Ocean was rough at times but I felt safe on board the large cruise liner and visited many of the bars and restaurants on board the ship. During this time I was travelling as a single person, but had no difficulty in mixing with other people on the cruise who were mostly British and with the supreme self-confidence of my manic bipolar high, including the staff and crew some of who were Pilipino and they were very friendly and sociable as well and went out of their way to make me and fellow travellers feel comfortable despite the lengthy Trans-Atlantic crossing.

The 2nd cruise I took in the Caribbean was over a year later, when I flew direct to Barbados from Newcastle airport which took only nine hours avoiding the extra flight to and from Southampton, and was probably a more comfortable ride and speedy way to travel to Barbados than my previous cruise to Madeira and across the whole of the Atlantic Ocean.

Barbados was one of the larger, if not the largest islands we visited and was the starting point of our cruise around the Caribbean. It was partially very commercialised and, in some parts, industrialised but the port at which I joined the cruise ship at Bridgetown was comparatively very clean and lovely from which we set sail on both cruises over a year apart.

The weather was glorious in the Caribbean Sea and Leeward and Windward seas around which we cruised which were generally calm, with the occasional mild storm lasting only a few hours and most of the time we had lovely warm sunshine from dawn to dusk.

Even if I had not been high with my bipolar during my Caribbean cruises, I would have been high on life itself, viewing the stunning scenery, beautiful azure seas and characterful islands that we visited or revisited. The 1st of which was Antigua and Barbuda, with its joyful palms, beaches, beautiful restaurants and bars comparatively un-spoilt virginal tourist, less sandy bays on which all manner of seagoing sail boats, motor launches, speed boats and private yachts were moored and bobbed in the gentle sea swell. The port that we anchored in was called St Johns and I visited this island on both cruises much to my pleasure.

The next islands we visited were called St Kitts and the port was called Basseterre and these islands were less commercialised than Antigua and apparently un-spoilt and the views were just as beautiful and scenic as was Antigua. We had roughly a day to tour the islands on a number of organised trips to appreciate the full beauty of different character of each of the Caribbean islands we visited.

We would often take day trips around islands we were fully accommodated on board the cruise ship and generally had two meals a day, breakfast and dinner in the beautiful restaurants on board the ship, and often visiting one of the theatres for shows including singing and dancing in the bars until late in the evening.

The next island we visited on both cruises was the British Virgin Islands, for which the port was Tortola and was seemingly equally as impressive as the 1st two islands we visited, with beautiful seascapes, ocean views, marvellous sandy or some areas rock strewn, pebbly beaches and beach bars friendly enticing cafes and restaurants.

Next we spent a further day at sea enjoying the luxury of a cruise ship until we arrive at Grand Turk of the Turks and Cacaos islands which was although more commercialised than other islands we had been to, was still breathtakingly beautiful and the we either took organised tours of the island or set off individually to explore bars, cafes, restaurants, shops on the island. We spent a further day at sea cruising until reaching St Maarten in which the port was Phillipsburg another characterful and beautiful island with beautiful seascapes and landscapes, plenty of bars and restaurants to choose from.

The next island we visited, possibly the most beautiful of all, was St Lucia for which the port was Castries with fabulous views of the harbours sweeping bays, beaches, commercial activities and very interesting traveller's shops with all sorts of nick knacks, art souvenirs and local handicrafts.

The penultimate island that we visited was on the second cruise only, which was Grenada, for which the port was called St Georges, on which I took a boat tour around the island but unfortunately my Panama hat blew off my head with the wind in the dock and ended up in the Caribbean Sea much to my chagrin as I loved that hat. Yet fortunately, I met a local chap and we got talking and when I told him my sad story in one of the sea bars, promptly wove me a Panama style hat made out of lemongrass and I still keep that hat to this day as a reminder of his generosity as all it cost me a bottle of beer with the marvellous conversation we had for over an hour as we talked about our lives and families and about the times on the beach as he was weaving my new hat, which I still keep to this day.

The next island we visited was St Vincent of which the port was called Kingstown and yet another beautiful island and aside from a few more beers in the beautiful harbour and beach cafes was uneventful.

Returning to the cruise liner back to Bridgetown Barbados where we had 24 hours in Bridgetown and I took a tour of Barbados before catching the flight back to Newcastle airport on both my first and second cruises to the Caribbean and on returning to my home about 30 minutes from the airport and a much welcome period of relaxation and reflection on some marvellous memories of the cruises at home.

Despite my bipolar, which made me more confident and adventurous and talkative to strangers during my cruises, I have no regrets in travelling as a single person on the cruises, as I make friends easily and have never been short of interesting company and companionship which both the cruises provided in spades on reflection.

Chapter 15
My Hero Father

After my mother died at the ripe old age of 80 and my father who was living alone in his bungalow near Cleadon Village, Tyne & Wear, I took to visiting him regularly, normally on a Friday evening for a cup of tea and a chat and a bit of company for him and a catch up for me. He was still working and would carry on working up to the age of 93. He was a very ambitious and capable engineer building his company S&S Precision Engineering Limited in Washington Tyne & Wear which he started with my mother at the age of 59 and built up over the years with input from my late brother Bob in the earlier days and Bobs 2 sons David and Ian who later went on to inherit the company when my father died at the age of almost 95.

One such Friday evening I had a visited my father as usual for a cup of tea and a chat although sometimes he was not very talkative, but some good times we would talk about the family, old cars many of which I have bought with him going to Gateshead motor auctions and picking up old cars and then selling them on. I valued those Friday evenings when the auction was on when he and I would drive up to Gateshead to attend the auctions and sometimes pick up an old banger for doing it up and selling on, and we would usually call in at the

Red Lion Public House in West Boldon on the way home which was when I was 18 and onwards. We had shandy and a toasted cheese and tomato sandwich and I value these times looking back very dearly, as I was with my dad and we had lots to talk about as he was very supportive both spiritually, mentally and financially over the years before he died.

One particular Friday evening I called over for a chat and a cup of tea as usual and we were talking in the front room of his bungalow and watching a bit of TV, when I noticed that the kitchen was literally on fire and I could see the flames through the Perspex windows to the kitchen which gave me quite a shock and I shouted, 'My dad the house is on fire.' To which he swore, 'Bloody hell!' and we both dashed to the kitchen negotiating the flames in the various units which were burning and let ourselves out of the back door where it was dark outside apart from the flickering light of the flames.

To my surprise and later on, with great pride my father insisted on unravelling the garden hose in the back garden and struggled to connect it to the outside tap in the semi dark, then on a number of occasions going back into the blazing kitchen and tried to douse the flames with the spray from the hose. While I just stood back in awe just wondering whether he would get back out of the blazing bungalow each time he went in again and again.

One of the neighbours must have had called out the fire brigade and they arrived within a quarter of an hour but by that time most of the damage had been done to the house, particularly to the ground floor kitchen area and the fire brigade finally put all the flames out and the house was safe but in bad repair and stunk of smoke, a rank smell everywhere and was covered in a sooty substance which the fire men said was smoke damage.

As I look back to this dangerous time with great pride of my father whose courageous efforts as an old timer I realise we had been very lucky to have escaped, alive and unhurt and such courage was mentioned in the local paper the Shields' Gazette, who covered the story and pointed out that how that the fire had started as my father has left a candle burning inside his freezer to defrost it and the candle had finally melted the plastic inside the freezer and set alight causing the fire.

Afterwards, we realised that the bungalow was badly smoke damaged throughout and it needed a lot of work to re-fit the kitchen, clean up and re-decorate the rest of the property which was paid for by my father's home insurance. It could have been far worse had it not been for my father's quick thinking and courage.

Chapter 16
The Baltics

During one of my many bipolar highs I booked a cruise to the Baltics on Fred Olsen Lines sailing from my home port of Newcastle and across the North Sea to a number of ports in Continental Europe, 1st of all was Rotterdam which was a very large industrialised port, but typically Dutch with lots of cafes, bars and restaurants some of which I visited on my day trip around Rotterdam. Before setting sail for Denmark and more specifically Copenhagen port.

When arriving the next morning as we had sailed North overnight in the North Sea to Copenhagen in Denmark which was a very cosmopolitan city with lovely streets, restaurants, shops and cafes. Some of the passengers and I took a day trip on board a coach round the city to see the little mermaid statue for which Copenhagen is well known, finding it to be quite a small statue, only a few feet high but with a backdrop of a large bay behind it and a pause for photographs and snaps, as the views over the waterside city were magnificent. Again, the restaurants and cafes were very friendly and in particular to the English and there were no language problems, but they very much appreciated the English and were very friendly and affable even in the shops and other tourist areas.

From the port of Copenhagen, we cruised north up the Baltic Sea to Stockholm, Sweden, another very cosmopolitan and busy city and port and together with all the sights and sounds of the city, I found the Swedish were comparatively friendly with generally English spoken quite widely and the typical attitude of the Swedish being laid back very and cool and sophisticated. Stockholm is a marvellous city with lots of scenic and architectural beauty to occupy tourists and in essence very modern with lots of new space age buildings, factories, warehouses and shopping centres to attract business from both tourists and local Swedes.

After Stockholm we cruised across the Baltic Sea to the Gulf of Bothnia to enter the Gulf of Finland and passed Estonia onward to St Petersburg and Russia, which was definitely the highlight of the cruise, and was probably the most beautiful place I have ever seen in all of the cruises and travels I've taken so far. With marvellous buildings, some ancient some new. One of the older beautiful buildings which was the size of St Paul's Cathedral in London, but was extremely ornate and ancient was called the Romanoff's Winter Palace for the Tsar's and his family. The Winter Palace was very large an intricate on the outside but inside doubly so with every square inch of the massive inner walls and ceilings coated with ornate gold leaf, which was unbelievable to view and the memory of its splendour is clear and with me until this day.

Outside on the main road the Rue de Paris were various Russians mostly artists selling their works and I was happy to talk to them and view their paintings and prints of local scenes and was happy to purchase a few paintings from them for a few tens of Roupels, which I have kept until this day, as souvenirs of a marvellous city.

Even the police who being Russian were generally of a young age and were very friendly and affable and didn't carry guns, instead they had walkie talkies strapped to their waist. Not what I expected, due to the view I had previously of the military history and aggression. They were more than happy to act as tourist guides and far from the image we may have in England of Russians being authoritarian and autocratic and not so friendly, instead to my surprise even the police were very friendly and willing to help tourists find local land spots. They were nothing like the impressions of military superiority displayed by the massive parades annually in 400 miles south east in Moscow.

However, we were told to meet at the coach in which we had toured the city at a certain point in the city but not to stray too far from it into nearby streets and I took it, with my big bipolar self-confidence flowing, to try a few streets either side of where we had to meet. The restaurants were beautiful and the shops were second to none easily as good and as posh as the large shops in London. On this 'illegal' walk around the shops I spotted a bargain clothes shop and couldn't resist going in where amongst other clothes displayed was a Russian Fur hat with drop down ear covers on either side and a plastic police badge which I bought for a few Rouples and still have to this day.

St Petersburg was about four hundred miles from Moscow to the South East and friends of mine who had visited Moscow, told me later that they had visited on the days of the grand military procession through Moscow, a display of might and military power but none of this has ever been seen in St Petersburg which had a very light friendly international atmosphere to tourists.

Indeed St Petersburg became the highlight of the cruise despite the fact we had other places to call in on, on the way back from Russia and the next stop was the port of Tallinn, one of the ports of Estonia, which although previously had been part of the USSR was now an independent country and a member of the European Community. Estonia and Tallinn were great they had a lovely light atmosphere and many of the locals could speak English and I fully enjoyed touring the shops, cafes, restaurants and bars of Tallinn, which was my 2nd favourite city on the tour.

In Tallinn's high street I visited an antique shop which looked very interesting with local antiques on display and purchased some books of local stamps of about 100 in total, which I purchased for a few tens of Euro's and now form the base of my international stamp collection with their beautiful artwork both old and new.

The European Cruise home continued on next day voyaging back down the Baltic Sea passing Lithuania and Latvia on the port side until we eventually came to the coast of Germany where we promptly toured down the Kiel Canal after passing Kiel at the entrance of the man vast and impressive man made canal and travelled on this marvellous waterway for the best part of 60 miles passing all kinds of trade, factories, warehouses, farmland and the canal itself which had been cut and dug from the surrounding landscape and was about a thousand yards wide in most places and led us to shipyards, ports, storage warehouses on either side as we cruised through Germany on water, until we came to the town of Bremerhaven where we exited the German canal.

So back across the North Sea to my home port of Newcastle. Cruise over but feeling pretty high on life and in particular enjoying the many stops we had made over on the cruise and the many cities I had explored, with the proviso that St Petersburg was probably the most attractive city I have ever visited in my many years of holidays and cruises.

Chapter 17
The Solitair Years

In between the cruises in 2017 – 2019, and with still some of the funds I inherited from my father's estate remaining, my bipolar condition was evident again and with my supreme self-confidence that in my eyes for singles holidays, I booked two further specifically singles holidays with a specialist singles tour operator namely 'Solitair'.

One holiday to Tenerife in the Canaries and one to the isle of Ischia off Italy, more precisely off the Bay of Naples, and both were very enjoyable and because of the orientation towards single persons, were well organised and quite pleasant and exciting.

The first holiday for singles comprised of a flight from Newcastle airport direct to Tenerife South airport, where I met the other seven single persons who had the courage to travel independently and my self-confidence was growing throughout the holiday as I got to know the other seven single people, which comprised of 4 ladies and 4 men, making up the total group of eight people which included myself. My first impressions were good although all the singles were quite young, very much younger than myself, but they were all talkative and they chatted quite easily once the holiday had begun.

We travelled by minibus to our hotel in Porto de la Cruz in Tenerife in April 2019, of all the singles got to know each other gradually better, the various life stories and attitudes of each one of them came to life. Tenerife is a volcanic island and Porto del la Cruz is situated on the north edge of the island in the foothills of the volcanic peak, which influenced the weather greatly, and over the week we did not enjoy the 25 degrees weather which was over the rest of the island in April, as it drizzled or rained most of the week, due to its proximity in the high ground of the volcano where the clouds gathered in the spring time.

In the hotel gardens there was an entrance to the National Arboretum which was a large rugged area containing very many species of trees and plants in particular and these all thrived in the semi-sub tropic all round climate in the mountainous ground near to the volcano.

The singles, myself included, generally had meals together comprising of breakfast and evening meal for the half board accommodation in the hotel. So we had plenty of time to catch up on what activities each had been on during the day time or were about to go on after breakfast and gradually over the course of the week, we got to know each other pretty well. Despite half of the group being ladies and half being men, there was no evidence of any romantic alliances during the holiday, or even budding affairs. This aside, as I was particularly interested in developing romantic alliances, none of the ladies appeared to be my type and I was in any case the oldest in the group by far, at the tender age of 70, but mainly with my bipolar was very active and easily aroused in the bed department, but nothing came to fruition despite the fact that the ladies were all individually, very nice but for their various reasons in their lives had not booked a single holiday solely for sexual purposes. Anyway, I was the only single person in the group and others had existing relationships back home in the UK.

Partly because of the depressing and rainy weather in the north of the island, few of the ladies booked a coach, which was more or less a large taxi really, to travel down to the south of the island namely, Playa de las Americas and I included myself and the trip took roughly half an hour passing through very nice landscapes with some industrialization and agriculture, until we finally arrived at the Play de las America's, which in comparison to the rainy north of the island was bathed in bright warm sunshine, for the whole of the day we spent down there, enjoying the cafes, restaurants and sandy beaches. The trip back north to Porto de la Cruz was uneventful with the drab dreary weather awaiting us on our return.

I had enjoyed Tenerife and the singles company and at no time felt lonely on the island and when we had all said our goodbyes at the airport; we all flew home to the UK to lead our separate lives with warm memories of the friends we had been during our short holiday and I promised myself that I would probably go on another singles' holiday later on with Solitair.

About a year after my Tenerife singles holiday I booked another singles holiday with Solitair, this time to the glamorous island of Ischia off the Bay of Naples in Italy and in the following September, pre-covid, travelled with Solitair again on a singles holiday from Newcastle airport to Naples airport and from there by hydrofoil to the romantic island of Ischia, where I thought since my arrival that my dreams were coming true, as it was adjacent to and had views over Capri and Anna Capri, which my late wife Tricia and I had visited 48 years ago, when we met, the original Lancashire lass herself namely Gracie Fields in a convent in which she lived in her retirement and she sang her theme tune Sally, Sally Pride of Alley to her doting audience what was this time at her old age of 80 years, but she was quite friendly and approachable and made a bit of a fuss of the young couple Tricia and I. Capri was a magical island although very steep and hilly.

It was an exciting journey to Ischia and from the airport with a short ride by the Italian style small taxi which were called Piaggio's, down to the hydrofoil port, and from there about a 45-minute crossing to Ischia and the Continental Mare Hotel, which overlooked the coast and rugged rocks with views of Capri and Anna Capri and was beautiful. This time, there were only four singles in the group in total, 2 men, including myself, and 2 ladies, but they were good company and we enjoyed our meals together over the week as we explored parts of the islands including the beautiful harbour and docks area and lots of cafes and restaurants.

On one such skirmish, I spotted a property which I was captivated by in one of the Estate Agents or immobillaires' windows, which was a derelict building at one time, a villa called Rustico via Piano Liguori, Ischia, which, with my bipolar high at the time, I had to have and which was masterful to look at, really run down but beautiful. In a nutshell, I fell in love with it and imagined all kinds of plans and schemes to buy it and convert it into a restaurant, which I visualised would be called *Restaurant Conchita,* but needless to say, my offer was not accepted and it was sold in the following August, after my visit and offer in spring, much to my disappointment.

Another dream in tatters but in any case my three sons were dead set against me travelling back to Ischia and fulfilling my dream. Although, I tried to book two more recent holidays to Ischia but both were cancelled because of Covid-19, and my bipolar dream was dashed except by reacting my experience in writing this book, at least in part.

The weather was gorgeous with bright sunshine for the whole week in Ischia, and on the terrace of my hotel, The Hotel Continental Mere, I first started writing this book, *Bipolar Adventures,* as the atmosphere was so creative, peaceful, and the scenery and views were so beautiful, inspiring my writing, which has, thus far, been so relaxing and satisfying.

I have vowed to go back to Ischia one day, post Covid and to see what became of the derelict building Rustico via Piano, Liguori and whether someone else has fulfilled their dreams and converted it into a restaurant overlooking the Isles of Capri and Ana Capri in the most romantic setting.

Over the last two years, I have intended to take other singles holidays but unfortunately the company running them namely Solitair has gone bust as many travel companies have under Covid and we will just have to see if they re-start in future with a clear playing field for single travellers who desire a sense of freedom coupled with, company and companionship not possibly suffering from bipolar disorder and not having to boost to their self-confidence in meeting and mixing with other people in the same boat, but probably not due to my bipolar like me and potentially missing out on some great but creative highs on life times, during the cycle from high to low and to high again in their attitudes and outlook on life over time.